Paw Prints

Golden Retrievers

by Kaitlyn Duling

Bullfrog Books

Ideas for Parents and Teachers

Bullfrog Books let children practice reading informational text at the earliest reading levels. Repetition, familiar words, and photo labels support early readers.

Before Reading

- Discuss the cover photo. What does it tell them?

- Look at the picture glossary together. Read and discuss the words.

Read the Book

- "Walk" through the book and look at the photos. Let the child ask questions. Point out the photo labels.

- Read the book to the child, or have him or her read independently.

After Reading

- Prompt the child to think more. Ask: Have you ever seen a golden retriever? Do you want to play with one?

Bullfrog Books are published by Jump!
5357 Penn Avenue South
Minneapolis, MN 55419
www.jumplibrary.com

Copyright © 2019 Jump! International copyright reserved in all countries. No part of this book may be reproduced in any form without written permission from the publisher.

Library of Congress Cataloging-in-Publication Data

Names: Duling, Kaitlyn, author.
Title: Golden retrievers / by Kaitlyn Duling.
Description: Minneapolis, MN : Jump!, Inc., 2018.
Series: Paw prints
Series: Bullfrog books | Includes index.
Audience: Ages 5 to 8. | Audience: Grades K to 3.
Identifiers: LCCN 2017041231 (print)
LCCN 2017043185 (ebook)
ISBN 9781624967757 (ebook)
ISBN 9781624967740 (hardcover : alk. paper)
Subjects: LCSH: Golden retriever—Juvenile literature.
Classification: LCC SF429.G63 (ebook)
LCC SF429.G63 D85 2018 (print) | DDC 636.752/7—dc23
LC record available at https://lccn.loc.gov/2017041231

Editor: Jenna Trnka
Book Designer: Molly Ballanger

Photo Credits: MilsiArt/Shutterstock, cover, 1; Eric Isselee/Shutterstock, 3; Olena Brodetska/Shutterstock, 4, 23ml; Mark Raycroft/Minden Pictures/SuperStock, 5; John Daniels/Pantheon/SuperStock, 6–7, 23bl; muratart/Shutterstock, 8–9; Jonathan Pledger/Shutterstock, 10–11; Linn Currie/Shutterstock, 12–13, 23tr; ColorBlind/Getty, 14; Ron Levine/Getty, 15; Jean Michel Labat/Pantheon/SuperStock, 16–17, 23tl; George Lamson/Shutterstock, 18; sonya etchison/Shutterstock, 19, 23br; andresr/iStock, 20–21; Lisa A. Svara/Shutterstock, 22; Ilucky78/Shutterstock, 23mr; ESB Professional/Shutterstock, 24.

Printed in the United States of America at Corporate Graphics in North Mankato, Minnesota.

Table of Contents

Good Swimmers

Look at that dog.

It is big.

Its tail is long.

It is a golden retriever!

5

See its long coat?

It is gold.

It shines.

coat ·····▶

It is also thick.
It helps them
stay warm.

Even in water.

These dogs love to swim!

They are from Scotland.
They were bred
to retrieve.

They help hunt.

13

These dogs are nice.

14

They like to listen
to their owners.

They work.

They help.

This one helps a woman who is blind.

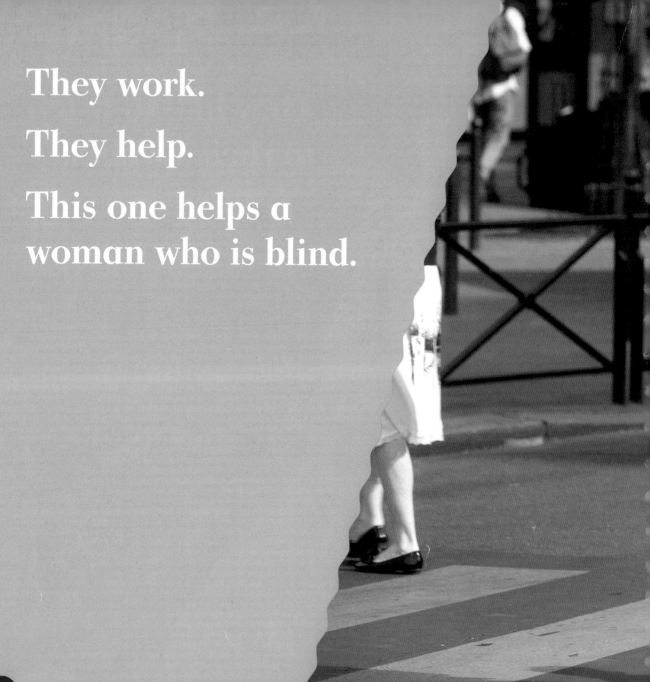

Golden retrievers like to play.

They run.

They fetch.

They like to learn tricks.

19

Do you want to
play with one?

A Golden Retriever Up Close

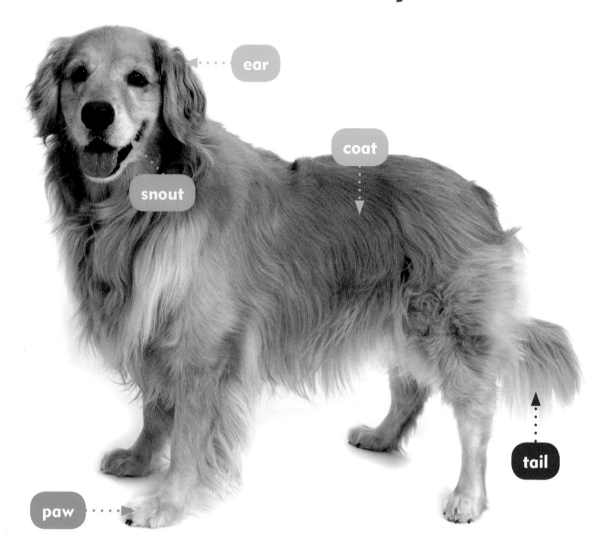

ear

coat

snout

tail

paw

Picture Glossary

blind
Unable to see.

retrieve
To get something and bring it back.

bred
Developed as a dog breed.

Scotland
A country in Northern Europe.

coat
A dog's fur.

tricks
Clever skills or actions dogs are trained to learn.

Index

To Learn More

Learning more is as easy as 1, 2, 3.

1) Go to www.factsurfer.com

2) Enter "goldenretrievers" into the search box.

3) Click the "Surf" button to see a list of websites.

With factsurfer.com, finding more information is just a click away.